WISHES OF AN ABSENT FATHER

SANTIEGO RIVERS

Wishes of an absent father

(My truth)

Copyright © 2021 by **Santiego Rivers**

All rights reserved. This book may not be reproduced or transmitted in any form without the written permission of the author.

ISBN: 978-1-7370516-3-3

There are decisions in life that we make that change who we are as a person. Sometimes doing the right thing can be the wrong thing for that other person. No one desires to be a bad parent or not be there for their child.

Sometimes we make decisions that we can't take back regardless of why we made the decision in the first place.

As a man, one of the greatest joys you can have is having your firstborn child. Your firstborn son becomes your namesake that will carry on your legacy.

Coming from a single-parent home, not having a male role model to emulate as a young boy puts a delay on you genuinely becoming a man.

Many single mothers have successfully raised solid male children, but there will always be something missing in that boy's life when the father is not present in their life.

How does a male child raised by a single mother learn how to be a man? Who teaches that child the responsibility of man and how a man should carry themselves in life?

Does not being present in the child's life become the vicious cycle that the son carries on? When does the cycle end? In this book, I will shed light on the biggest mistake that I made in my life and take full ownership of my decision.

This book will tell you the struggles that I had being a parent despite my desire to be the best parent that I could be. My goal was to break the cycle that I was born into but only succeed in continuing it.

The best way to change or break any cycle is by first admitting a need for change. I want my children not to make the same mistakes that I made as a parent. Even a lousy parent can teach a child valuable lessons from their mistakes.

I never claimed to be perfect, but I am willing to take ownership of all the mistakes I made and make in my life. One of the most important lessons that a parent hopefully learns is that your child does not need you to be perfect; they need you to be present in their life, even when they think that they don't.

Growing up in a single-parent home was tough for me. But after getting to know my father and his flaws as a man, I realized that I grew up around people who would best suit the person I was inside.

When you grow up without having certain things you want in your life, it shapes your future without knowing. My mother raised me, but I was always searching for a home with a male role model in it as a child.

I spent a lot of time at both of my grandparent's homes and family members that had men inside the house. However, as I reflect on my childhood, this searching for a father figure occurred when I realized that my home did not have one.

My mother had men that she dated, but none of them felt like a father to me. The person whom I thought was my father turned out not to be him. The happiest I remember my childhood being was when my mother was with the man who allowed us not to struggle in life.

It was amazing to see a man coming home from work and how he greeted his wife as a male child. I loved how the wife would have his food ready for him and made sure that the house was in order when he came home. I loved the little things inside a marriage that makes the union beautiful.

Having a family has always been one of the things that I have always wanted as a child. This desire for a family had driven me to make some bad decisions even when I thought I was doing what was right. I loved the examples that my family showed me as a child.

I understand that this was a different time in life, but people knew how to make the other person feel loved, respected & appreciated. Therefore, I loved growing up in my era before standards, morals, and respect went out of the window.

Seeing how men operated inside a family made me desire to be that type of man when I grew up. There were many things that I did not do as a child that I probably would have taken a greater interest in if I had a male authority figure in the house. Being a single parent takes you away from doing and participating in many activities that your child has.

I never played any organized sports until I reached high school because I didn't have a male role model who nurtured my ability and taught me how to work for what I wanted in life.

I got into sports by following the friends in my neighborhood who attended the same school as me. However, I did not take sports seriously because I still struggled with learning my identity.

You never know how much not having a missing parent in your life can affect the decisions and choices that you make in life.

For kids who do not have a male role model inside the home, your coaches become the men you look up to.

As a child, I wanted to become the type of man that my child would one day look up to. I wanted to become the type of father/man that I could even admire.

I was good at sports, but I knew that playing sports was not something I wanted to do for the rest of my life. Instead, I was a thinker who needed to find my voice to express my deepest feelings. So, I fell in love with writing poetry at an early age.

Writing allowed me to touch and nurture the part of my soul that needed to be heard. I was fortunate to find a male friend who also loved writing and expressing himself with written words. Ironically, he is still one of the few friends I still communicate with from my childhood.

My childhood left me with many holes in my character and structure as a man, but it never left me not wanting to one day become a father myself.

As a child, you wonder why a parent would choose to play such a minimal role in their child's life. The other parent would often paint a negative picture of the other parent or try to fill the missing void. Sometimes the situation that takes the parent out of the child's life is for the best of the child.

Either way, I feel that a loved one should have a conversation with that child to help them understand why the other parent is missing from their life. I have learned that male children often tend to act out when they realize that the male figure who was supposed to shape and mold them into a man is missing out on their lives.

Many feelings go through a child's mind when they wonder why that other parent is not present in their life. Not having a father in my home did not help with my self-esteem issues, confidence & development as a man.

On a few occasions, I did have a chance to live with my father, but I was not ready to accept the things happening under his roof.

As a child longing for his father's time and attention, my father did not measure up to what I thought I was missing from my life.

Just because a man fathers a child does not always mean that he will develop into a good dad. I am a perfect example of this philosophy.

 Over the years, I have learned that broken people tend to break others because they are hurting and broken themselves.

After graduating from high school, I was fortunate enough to have my first child, but that did not mean that I was ready to become a parent.

I was still learning who I was as a person and what direction my life will be heading. In addition, I was dealing with demons that still haunted me late into my adult years.

Bearing my soul:

I did not expect to be alive this long in my life. But, unfortunately, my upbringing and feelings left me in a suicidal state that made me fantasize about taking my life because I had yet to learn how precious life is and the reason for my existence.

Before the birth of my first child, I had just gotten out of a relationship with a woman I wanted to be my wife. But, unfortunately, I was mentally in the wrong place. I was having one-night stands with women because my fiancé had cheated on me and broken my heart.

I was ready to be in a committed relationship and raise a family with a child who was not mine biologically, but she was not at a place in her life that she wanted the same thing.

That was the first serious relationship that had me looking forward to the future, even with my suicidal mind. After that, I did not care about anyone or anything.

If the woman I had my first child with did not end up pregnant, I seriously doubt that I would still be alive today. When I found out that I would have my first child, many emotions ran through my head.

I experienced moments of joy, sadness, anger, and calm thinking about me becoming a father. I had played the father in my previous relationship, and I was ready to continue that role with my first biological child despite not knowing anything about the mother.

I met my son's mother at Tyrone mall. The mall was the place where everyone went to meet other people when I was younger. So, she and I exchanged telephone numbers and made plans to hook up later.

She lived in Merritt Island, on the outskirts of Orlando. I planned to drive down there one weekend and make a memory. Instead, I ended up making a memory and a child.

Once I found out that I had a child, I told my family. It's incredible how it seems that all black people know each other. My family knew her family.

My family was very supportive and helped all that they could. I was starting my job with the school system as a teacher aide and wrestling coach.

I wouldn't say I liked that my son would be so far away, so I asked his mother to move in with me to be a part of his life.

I did not care if we were in a relationship or not; I just wanted to be there for my child. In addition, I felt that we would have a stronger support system and family in my hometown.

Unfortunately, having her move in with me never occurred. I used to send money to help, and my family sent packages as well. I admit that it was never a lot of money that I sent, but I sent what I could.

I was still in a volatile state of living during that time. I ended up getting another woman pregnant while I was expecting my first child.

Supposedly, the mother of my second child was on birth control when she became pregnant. I could have used a condom to protect myself and prevent becoming another parent before I was ready. Instead, I was having two babies by two different women.

I like to think of myself as a one-woman man, so this whole situation did not feel comfortable. I spent twenty years off-and-on with my daughters' mom because I wanted a family and wanted to be present in at least one of my children's lives.

It made it hard being there for my son during being with my daughters' mom. I take full blame/ responsibility for not being as involved in my son's life.

I hoped that things would get better over time, but sometimes things do not work out the way you desire. They say that when man plans, the Most High laugh. I understand why.

My son mother put me on child support that complicated my life. I understand and accept what happened because I could have and should have done more. She should not have had to raise our son on her own.

I had my licenses suspended, and I was getting arrested for driving with suspended licenses regularly for falling behind on child support.

The type of work that I did to earn a living required me to drive on the regular. With not being able to be a part of my son's life because they were moving out of state and me being one more arrest from facing prison time, I did something that I regret to this day.

My son's mother was getting married, and she asked if her new husband could adopt my son. Honestly, I did not know how to feel.

In my mind, the paper that she wanted me to sign did not mean that he is not my son. So, I weighed the pros and cons of signing my rights over to another man.

The pros of letting someone adopt my child

- My son would know how it feels to have two parents in the same household.
- My son would have a male role model in his life.
- My son would have a man in his life who could financially take care of him.
- He was going to have a step-father regardless.
- I would be taken off child support by signing the paper.
- I could get my licenses back
- I did not have to worry about going to prison.
- I did not have to worry about getting kicked out of the house in my current relationship because I wanted to spend time with my son.

The cons of letting someone adopt my child

- My son would carry someone else last name.
- I would miss having my son know how much I love him.
- I would miss seeing him grow up and getting to know me.

Many cons would develop after I signed the papers. As a young adult, you do not always realize all the consequences of making adult decisions.

I did not think about how my son would feel that I signed the papers to let him be adopted. I did not think about how I would feel that I did not fight more to be a part of his life.

I made a tough choice for many different reasons. Some of the reasons were for my benefit, but the core of my reasoning was for my son to have a life that I never had and could not give him at the current time.

Would I do the same thing again if I had the opportunity? With my current mindset, the answer would be no, but I realize that I made a tough decision based on the mentality of a broken child.

I was never taught how to fight for what I wanted. I grew up feeling so helpless and unworthy of love that I let people who said they love me take advantage of me.

I was currently younger than the age my son is now when I became a father. I was not even old enough to drink alcohol, yet I had two kids. As I watch my son's life from afar, I see someone on the same path that I was on around his age.

I see my son living for today, not thinking about tomorrow. All I see is the same cycle that I was a part of for most of my life.

Life has taught me that many things will become evident if you are blessed with enough time to live your life. Life will give you clarity that youth is not fortunate to always see.

As a parent, I understand now why my parents made so many mistakes as parents.

They were kids having kids while still trying to figure out their place in life.

Imagine having a child with someone you barely know. But, unfortunately, the lessons that we try to teach our children are the same lessons that we wished we had learned at their age.

Wisdom is a gift that time grants to those that are fortunate enough to learn the value of.

The following are the wishes that a father would want for their child/children to know. The following is what I would need for my son to know:

Be a better parent/ person than I ever was. I made many mistakes in my life, but having you was never one of them. I have loved you from the moment that I knew you existed.

I would trade and sacrifice my life for you and you're well-being. With every fiber in my being, you will always mean the world to me.

There is not one day or moment that you were not on my mind. So I kept, and I cherished every photo that I had of you.

I hope, and I pray that one day you will find/ discover your purpose in life. Stop wasting your time living in the moment and learn to start planning for tomorrow.

I wish you knew this version of me instead of the version of me that was not ready to be the dad you needed. If you are willing to get to know me, it may answer questions about yourself that you have yet to even think about.

Every day I try to become the best version of myself that you and your sisters would one day be proud of.

My struggles as a man affected my ability to be the dad you needed in your life. I hope to one day to be a part of your life.

I had to get to know my father so that I can have peace in my soul. I hope that one day you will feel the same way before your heart grows too cold.

Before you have a child, make sure that the person you are going to have a child with is willing to spend the rest of their life with you.

If you have a child already, break the cycle of not being present in your child's life. Use my bad examples of being a dad to become the prime example of what a dad should be.

Make sure the person you are going to have a child with is the person who challenges you to become the best version of yourself. Looks should never be the reason that you are willing to have a child with someone.

Get to know yourself first before you decide to bring anyone into your life. Learn what you are willing to accept and live with before you lower your standards.

Sacrifice your pride to obtain all the things that you truly desire in life. Understand the difference between wants and needs.

Learn to love and respect your mom. A wife should judge a man on how he treats his mother, and a husband should judge his woman how she respects and treats her father.

A woman needs to feel loved, a man needs to feel respected.

They say you can learn a lot from a dummy, so this dummy is here to help you learn from his mistakes.

www.ingramcontent.com/pod-product-compliance
Lightning Source LLC
Chambersburg PA
CBHW071014160426
43193CB00012B/2052